Rebuild

The need for revival and restoration in the church

John Caldwell

Copyright © 2019 John Caldwell

All rights reserved.

ISBN: 9781092493710

DEDICATION

To fellow fire-brands.

CONTENTS

	Acknowledgments	i
1	THE CHURCH: A RUINED HOUSE?	8
2	CATCHING A VISION OF REVIVAL AND RESTORATION	26
3	REBUILDING THE HOUSE	42
4	CAN THESE BONES LIVE?	61

ACKNOWLEDGMENTS

Unlike most of my other books, the chapters in this book began as stand-alone messages that were preached in various churches and Christian gatherings in Scotland. From this perspective I'd like to thank the various leaders and congregations who welcomed both the message and the messenger. The encouragement received from these Christians was the catalyst that caused me to put the messages in to book form.

1

THE CHURCH: A RUINED HOUSE? (ISAIAH 56)

And the Lord will continually guide you,

And satisfy your desire in scorched places,

And give strength to your bones;

And you will be like a watered garden,

And like a spring of water whose waters do not fail.

"Those from among you will rebuild the ancient ruins;

You will raise up the age-old foundations;

And you will be called the repairer of the breach,

The restorer of the streets in which to dwell.

(Isaiah 56:11-12)

Isaiah's prophecies pointed forward to the soon coming judgement of Israel. Israel's unfaithfulness would ultimately lead to the ransacking of Israel; the destruction of the temple; and the captivity of God's people. However, Isaiah's prophecies also predicted a future restoration. Today, in the Western world, in many ways, God's house lies in ruins and many of His people are bound in captivity. Yet the Lord still has a purpose for his church. In these days of spiritual decline, the Lord is looking for those who will hear and obey the call to raise up the ancient foundations and rebuild the ancient ruins.

God had a purpose for his people Israel. He had set them apart, blessed them, and called them to be a blessing to the nations:

> You will be like a watered garden, And like a spring of water whose waters do not fail. (Isaiah 58:11)

In a world that is labouring under the curse of the fall, God's people are called to be a source of refreshing and restoration. In a world that is full of darkness, the Lord said to his people:

> 'I will make you a light to the nations.'

However, in the context of this passage, Israel has a major problem: they are missing it big time! Israel's failure was specifically due to idolatry, worldliness, rejecting God's word and continually ignoring the prophets.

As a consequence of Israel's sin, the nation would be attacked; the protective walls of the city would be broken down; Israel and Jerusalem would be ransacked; the temple would be destroyed (even the foundations) and Israel and Judah would be taken into captivity.

These events are not just historical stories that have no relevance for the church today. The New Testament teaches us the purpose of these events within the Old Testament scriptures:

> Now these things happened to them as an example, and they were written for our instruction, upon whom the ends of the ages have come. (1 Cor 10:11)

God's purpose for Israel was revealed in our opening text: "You will be like a watered garden, And like a spring of water whose waters do not fail." In other words, the church was called to be a source of refreshing and restoration in a parched and barren world. This purpose was not just for Israel, it also applies to the church today. It is comparable to Jesus' statement when he said:

"He who believes in Me, as the Scripture said, 'From his innermost being will flow rivers of living water.' (John 7:38)

In the book of Joel and Acts the Lord declared: 'I will pour out my Spirit, in the last days...' Yet the tragedy of our times is that in many places, the rains have stopped, the river is no longer flowing, and the wells have been blocked.

J.N Darby, the founder of the Brethren movement, referred to the church as: 'The House of Ruins.' Darby was drawing from the imagery of the ruined temple in the Old Testament. Why did Darby think in these terms? He perceived that many essential truths had been lost to the church and that the church was in a terrible condition.

We can see from both biblical history and church history that the church has often ended up in a condition of ruin and disgrace. This is why the apostle John warned the church against the snare of the world:

> Do not love the world or the things in the world. If anyone loves the world, the love of the Father is not in him. 16 For all that is in the world—the desires of the flesh and the desires of the eyes and pride of life[c]—is not from the Father but is from the world. (1 John 2:

15)

James Montgomery Boice, in his book, 'What Happened to the Gospel of Grace?' demonstrates that many churches seem to reflect the world's values, such as humanism, which says: 'It's all about people and their potential'; individualism which makes it about 'Me and my rights' (this is especially true in the context of evangelical biblical interpretation where individual interpretations triumph over traditional interpretations); pragmatism which makes Christianity focus on whatever works instead of whatever is true and hedonism which makes personal happiness is the ultimate goal.

Consequently the world's entertainment has become the true god of many professing believers. Music, sports and TV have become the modern idols. As a consequence worldliness has affected many believers' mind-set, conversation, lifestyle and religion. As a result, many believers are missing out on God's purpose and blessing:

> And the LORD will continually guide you, And satisfy your desire in scorched places, And give strength to your bones; And you will be like a watered garden, And like a spring of water whose waters do not fail. (Isaiah 58:11)

Instead of knowing and enjoying God's guidance, satisfaction, and strength, they lack purpose; they feel like something is missing in their walk with God and they are weak and weary.

This is exactly the situation that Israel was in and it is into these circumstances that God gave His people a promise. God promises to raise up a people who will rebuild the ancient ruins:

> Those from among you will rebuild the ancient ruins; You will raise up the age-old foundations; And you will be called the repairer of the breach, The restorer of the streets in which to dwell. (Isaiah 58:12)

For Israel, this was fulfilled through: Nehemiah, Ezra, Haggai, Zerubbabel and Joshua. However, the call of Haggai is also a call to the church today:

> Thus says the LORD of hosts, 'This people says, "The time has not come, even the time for the house of the LORD to be rebuilt." (Haggai 1:2)

This is reinforced by the words of Jesus concerning His church:

I will build my church, and the gates of Hades will not overcome it. (Matt 16:18)

How is Jesus building his church today? I believe the answer is revealed in the book of Ephesians.

Eph 4:7-16

[7] But to each one of us grace was given according to the measure of Christ's gift.

[8] Therefore it says,

"WHEN HE ASCENDED ON HIGH,

HE LED CAPTIVE A HOST OF CAPTIVES,

AND HE GAVE GIFTS TO MEN."

[9] (Now this expression, "He ascended," what does it mean except that He also had descended into the lower parts of the earth? [10] He who descended is Himself also He who ascended far above all the heavens, so that He might fill all things.) [11] And He gave some as apostles, and some as prophets, and some as evangelists, and some as pastors and teachers, [12] for the equipping of the saints for the work of

service, to the building up of the body of Christ; [13]until we all attain to the unity of the faith, and of the knowledge of the Son of God, to a mature man, to the measure of the stature which belongs to the fullness of Christ. [14]As a result, we are no longer to be children, tossed here and there by waves and carried about by every wind of doctrine, by the trickery of men, by craftiness in deceitful scheming; [15]but speaking the truth in love, we are to grow up in all aspects into Him who is the head, even Christ, [16]from whom the whole body, being fitted and held together by what every joint supplies, according to the proper working of each individual part, causes the growth of the body for the building up of itself in love.

The ascended Christ has poured out His Spirit upon believers, the Spirit is the living presence of Christ in the Church, God's purpose in this is that Christ might have expression through the church as the outpoured Spirit releases spiritual gifts to all believers. As every believer is aligned with God's purpose and carries out the work of ministry, the church grows and comes to maturity. Therefore the church grows as every believer finds their place in the purpose of God and Jesus is revealed more fully through the ministry of the word and the equipping of the saints for service.

However, there are scriptural warnings which we need to pay attention to when it comes to the work of building: the church is God's, not ours. We live in a generation which is obsessed with the newest thing. God's people are called to rebuild the ancient ruins not construct a modern monument! Ephesians warns about the church being 'blown about by every wind of false doctrine', yet there are no end to the fads which blow through the modern church. The scriptures are clear: 'Unless the Lord builds the house, they who build labour in vain.' How is it possible to labour in vain? We can labour in vain in a number of ways, but one of the key ways that we labour in vain is when we build on the wrong foundations.

God is looking for a people who will rebuild the age-old foundations:

> When Jesus came to the region of Caesarea Philippi, he asked his disciples, "Who do people say the Son of Man is?" They replied, "Some say John the Baptist; others say Elijah; and still others, Jeremiah or one of the prophets." "But what about you?" he asked. "Who do you say I am?" Simon Peter answered, "You are the Christ, the Son of the living God." Jesus replied,

> "Blessed are you, Simon son of Jonah, for this was not revealed to you by man, but by my Father in heaven. And I tell you that you are Peter, and on this rock I will build my church, and the gates of Hades will not overcome it. (Matt 16:13-18).

The rock upon which Jesus Christ is building His church is the revelation that Jesus Christ is the Son of the Living God.

> For no one can lay any foundation other than the one already laid, which is Jesus Christ. (1 Cor 3:1)

The Christian Life can only be built upon a true revelation of Christ and the revelation of Christ is something that is God given and 'not revealed by man.'

Why do we have so many young people (not just young people) who make a profession of faith; go through the waters of baptism yet show very little spiritual fruit? Why are there so many churches with young people who are in love with world? It seems that many churches are filled with young people who play the church game until they are old enough to leave, and then leave as soon as they can. Some would claim the answer lies in better programmes. They say we need better youth programmes, or better discipleship courses. However, I would argue that the problem is much deeper than this. The problem is a foundational problem.

The problem largely relates to a misunderstanding of the true nature of Christian conversion and assurance. Many churches teach that conversion is *based upon* a profession of faith in Christ and that the evidence of salvation is a 'sinner's prayer'. Consequently, *assurance rests upon a profession of faith*. Yet this is a seriously faulty foundation:

> [21] "Not everyone who says to me, 'Lord, Lord,' will enter the kingdom of heaven, but only the one who does the will of my Father who is in heaven. [22] Many will say to me on that day, 'Lord, Lord, did we not prophesy in your name and in your name drive out demons and in your name perform many miracles?' [23] Then I will tell them plainly, 'I never knew you. Away from me, you evildoers!' (Matt 7:21-23)

These are the most haunting words that Jesus ever said. Can we see the implication? Simply confessing with our mouths that Jesus is Lord is no guarantee that we are saved. Jesus is clear, some people who profess him with their lips, and even do lots of religious works, will not be saved in the end – their conversion was false.

True conversion and assurance, on the other hand, need to be based *upon the finished work of Christ alone*. Our faith must rest upon who He is, what He has done and why He has done it. Jesus is the Son of the Living God; God incarnate who came from heaven to earth to take the place of sinners. His death on the cross is the means by which redemption is secured; God did for his people what his people could not do for themselves because of his great love.

True conversion and assurance is ultimately the work of the Holy Spirit and is often referred to as the new birth. It is the Holy Spirit who leads us to a personal conviction of sin; repentance from sin and the true faith that trusts in Christ alone.

The evidence of true conversion is a changed life (at the realm of the desires not just the confession). For many Christians, these things are experiential realities – but this is not the case for everyone who attends church.

In the book of Judges we see that the ways of God were not always preserved from generation to generation:

> [8] Then Joshua the son of Nun, the servant of the LORD, died at the age of

one hundred and ten... [10] All that generation also were gathered to their fathers; and there arose another generation after them who did not know the LORD, nor yet the work which He had done for Israel. (Judges 2:8-9).

This is one of the issues which we observe today, several generations have emerged who do not know the Lord. I remember an old Brethren preacher once saying:

> 'First generation Christians have the bible in their hearts; second generations have the bible in their head and third generation Christians have the bible in their book cases.'

Of course it is not as simple as that. And the dichotomy between heart and mind is not as clear cut as this quote suggests. However, the old Brethren preacher was highlighting the principle which is seen in Judges. Many people have grown up with strong Christian parents or grandparents yet they have not come to know the Lord for themselves.

The revivalist and social activist, William Booth foresaw the dry rot of spiritual decline setting in in his day. He predicted that succeeding generations would be marked by the following characteristics:

> "I consider that the chief dangers which confront the coming century will be religion without the Holy Ghost, Christianity without Christ, forgiveness without repentance, salvation without regeneration, politics without God, and heaven without hell."

A.W Tozer also identified the degenerating characteristics of evangelical spirituality in his day:

> If I see aright, the cross of popular evangelicalism is not the cross of the New Testament. It is, rather, a new bright ornament upon the bosom of a self-assured and carnal Christianity. The old cross slew men, the new cross entertains them. The old cross condemned; the new cross amuses. The old cross destroyed confidence in the flesh; the new cross encourages it.

Was Booth wrong in his prediction? Was Tozer's problem restricted to his own times? What is the present condition of the Church of Jesus Christ? One pastor says:

> Assurance has always been a vitally important subject, but it is even more so now because we live in a day of minimal assurance. The main fruits of assurance, such as desire for fellowship with God, yearning for his glory and heaven, a godly walk of obedience, and

intercession for missions and revival, appear to be waning among contemporary Christians. This stems from the modern pulpit's emphasis on earthly happiness supplanting the conviction that we are pilgrims traveling through this world on our way to God and glory. [1]

Another contemporary leader says:

We believe that the major disease of the church today is JDD: Jesus Deficit Disorder. The person of Jesus is increasingly politically incorrect, and is being replaced by the language of "justice," "the kingdom of God," "values," and "leadership principles.

If this is true, then one of the greatest needs of the church is a restoration of the centrality of Christ. Is this not the nature of revival? What is revival if it is not a rediscovery of the living reality of Jesus? Revival is simply revisiting the cross of Christ. Coming to the cross should be similar to Isaiah's experience:

> In the year that King Uzziah died, I saw the Lord, high and exalted, seated on a throne; and the train of his robe filled the temple. Above him were seraphim, each

---

[1] R.C Sproul, *Assured By God*

with six wings: With two wings they covered their faces, with two they covered their feet, and with two they were flying. And they were calling to one another:

"Holy, holy, holy is the Lord Almighty;
the whole earth is full of his glory."

At the sound of their voices the doorposts and thresholds shook and the temple was filled with smoke.

"Woe to me!" I cried. "I am ruined! For I am a man of unclean lips, and I live among a people of unclean lips, and my eyes have seen the King, the Lord Almighty."

Then one of the seraphim flew to me with a live coal in his hand, which he had taken with tongs from the altar. With it he touched my mouth and said, "See, this has touched your lips; your guilt is taken away and your sin atoned for."

Then I heard the voice of the Lord saying, "Whom shall I send? And who will go for us?"

And I said, "Here am I. Send me!" (Isaiah 6: 1-8).

Isaiah testifies: 'I saw the Lord', he gets a glimpse of God in His glory. A glimpse of God results in a conviction of sin which leads to repentance. At the heart of his experience is a type and shadow of the atonement achieved by Christ's sacrifice. For the Christian, a true encounter with God will be a cleansing experience.

The outcome of a fresh encounter with Christ results in a fresh commission: "Whom shall I send? And who will go for us?"

The Lord is still looking for a people who will go. But before we can go, we must come — we must come to Christ for fresh cleansing and empowering.

When we look at the church and society today it is clear that there is a need for those who will be repairers of walls and restorers of streets with dwellings. Walls were the means of protecting cities from enemy attacks, when the enemy broke through the walls the city was destroyed.

> The thief comes only to steal and kill and destroy; I have come that they may

have life, and have it to the full." John 10:10

The enemy is creating havoc in people's lives. People are broken and in need of the restoration which can only come through the gospel.

> "You shall raise up the foundations of many generations; you shall be called the repairer of the breach, the restorer of streets to dwell in. (Isa 58:11)

There is a call to renew our vision of Christ and re-align our hearts with God's purpose. There is no guarantee that society will change in our lifetime, but we can take responsibility for our own lives. We can take responsibility for the local church. As individuals and congregations seek God and his purpose afresh, we will already be in the process of restoration, renewal and revival.

2

CATCHING A VISION OF REVIVAL AND RESTORATION (ZECHARIAH 4)

And the angel who talked with me came again and woke me, like a man who is awakened out of his sleep. ² And he said to me, "What do you see?" I said, "I see, and behold, a lampstand all of gold, with a bowl on the top of it, and seven lamps on it, with seven lips on each of the lamps that are on the top of it. ³ And there are two olive trees by it, one on the right of the bowl and the other on its left." ⁴ And I said to the angel who talked with me, "What are these, my lord?" ⁵ Then the angel who talked with me answered and said to me, "Do you not know what these are?" I said, "No, my lord." ⁶ Then he said to me, "This is the word of the Lord to Zerubbabel: Not by might, nor by power, but by my Spirit, says the Lord of hosts. ⁷ Who are you, O great mountain? Before Zerubbabel you shall become a plain. And he shall bring forward the top stone amid shouts of 'Grace, grace to it!'"

8 Then the word of the Lord came to me, saying, **9** "The hands of Zerubbabel have laid the foundation of this house; his hands shall also complete it. Then you will know that the Lord of hosts has sent me to you. **10** For whoever has despised the day of small things shall rejoice, and shall see the plumb line in the hand of Zerubbabel.

² And he said to me, "What do you see?"

What do *you* see, when you look at:

- The church?
- Your life?
- Your potential in God?
- Your community?
- The world?

Zechariah and Zerubbabel would have seen *rubble and ruins.* Rubble and ruins which were: a reminder of past failure; evidence of an impossible task; a source of discouragement and sign of their own weakness and inability.

God often asks his people this question "what do you see?"

What do we see?

As God's people we have a choice: will we look at our circumstances naturally, or supernaturally? Will we focus on what the devil's doing, or on what God is doing? Will our vision be limited by our own understanding, or will it be enlarged through the eyes of faith?

The context of Zechariah is the apostasy of Israel, the destruction of Jerusalem/Temple, the Babylonian captivity, and the call to return and build. During this period, the prophetic ministry of Zechariah and Haggai was pivotal in the process of rebuilding and Zerubbabel is the man commissioned and raised up to rebuild the temple of God – the place where God's glory rests.

However, Israel, not only needed to be rebuilt, *the people* needed to be revived and renewed.

Zech 4:1-8 reveals a number of principles of renewal and revival that are applicable to God's people today. In this chapter we will explore some of these principles.

1) We need a spiritual awakening

4 And the angel who talked with me came again and <u>woke me</u>, like a man who is <u>awakened</u> out of his sleep.

Bible dictionaries define the word AWAKE and AWAKENED in the following ways:

- "To awake, stir up, rouse oneself"
- "Commonly signifies <u>waking up out of an ordinary sleep</u>" (This is the literal meaning.)

> • "Its first use in the O.T has the sense of *"rousing" someone to action:* "Awake, awake Deborah." Judges 5:12"

What happens to Zechariah in the natural is what needs to happen to the people of Israel in the spiritual. Zechariah is asleep and is awakened by the Lord, Israel are spiritually asleep and need to be awakened. The people of God were in a place of slumber and needed to be awakened.

> Haggai 1: The word of the Lord came by the hand of Haggai the prophet to Zerubbabel the son of Shealtiel, governor of Judah, and to Joshua the son of Jehozadak, the high priest: *² "Thus says the Lord of hosts: These people say the time has not yet come to rebuild the house of the Lord." ³ Then the word of the Lord came by the hand of Haggai the prophet, ⁴ "Is it a time for you yourselves to dwell in your paneled houses, while this house lies in ruins?...* ¹⁴ **And the Lord stirred up the spirit of Zerubbabel** the son of Shealtiel, governor of Judah, and the spirit of Joshua the son of Jehozadak, the high priest, and the spirit of all the remnant of the people. And they came and worked on the house of the Lord of hosts, their God,

It is no coincidence that the word 'to awaken' Appears 80 times in the Old Testament. The New Testament also has a lot to say about spiritual sleep and the importance of being awake or awakened.

- Parable of the 10 virgins.
- Eph 5:14 Therefore it says, "Awake, O sleeper, and arise from the dead, and Christ will shine on you."
- 1 Thess 5:5 So then let us not sleep, as others do, but let us keep awake and be sober.

Sleep speaks of a number of things:

- Complacency
- Apathy
- Carelessness
- Comfort and compromise

AW Tozer said, "Christians don't tell lies, but they sing them all the time." The churches sing, "Jesus all for Jesus" but if we were more honest, we would be singing Pink Floyd's "I've become *comfortably numb.*"

Israel was preoccupied with their own lives and building their own homes, while God's house lay in ruins. History shows that the church often finds itself in need of revival and renewal. Someone once described the process in the following way: God raises up a man, the man births a movement, the movement becomes an institution, the institution becomes a monument and finally the monument becomes a museum. The Western and European landscapes are littered with empty ecclesiastical monuments which speak of a former glory and present demise.

No wonder John Darby saw the church as 'The house of ruins'! 'House of Ruins' is a relevant description for the western church today.

Consequently, as individuals, or churches, we can find ourselves in a place of slumber and in need of awakening.

The language of awakening is also used in the passage concerning Cyrus:

> "In the first year of Cyrus king of Persia, that the word of the Lord by the mouth of Jeremiah might be fulfilled, the Lord stirred up the spirit of Cyrus king of Persia."

Zechariah, as a book, is about a movement of the Spirit of God bringing about a movement of revival and restoration – and the Lord is not just stirring up and awakening his people – he is stirring up and awakening the lost. Charles Finney put it this way:

> "When sinners are careless and stupid, and sinking into hell unconcerned, it is time the church should bestir themselves. It is as much the duty of the church to awake, as it is for the firemen to awake when a fire breaks out in the night in a great city."

All of us whether we are believers, or unbelievers, need an awakening – we need to hear God's alarm clock:

> Zech 1: 3-4: Return to me, says the Lord of hosts, and I will return to you, says the Lord of hosts. [4] Do not be like your fathers, to whom the former prophets cried out, 'Thus says the Lord of hosts, Return from your evil ways and from your evil deeds.'

When the Lord awakens a person – to personal salvation or revival – it has a transforming effect. The person sees with a new set of eyes.

2) An awakening helps us see the church as God sees it

> *Zech 4:2 And he said to me, "What do you see?" I said, "I see, and behold, a lampstand all of gold, with a bowl on the top of it, and seven lamps on it, with seven lips on each of the lamps that are on the top of it.*

The lamp stand represents the church. We know this because scripture interprets scripture, and this is how the symbolism of the lampstand is interpreted in the book of Revelation.

> Rev 1:20 As for the mystery of the seven stars that you saw in my right hand, and the seven golden lampstands, the seven stars are the angels of the seven churches, and **the seven lampstands are the seven churches.**

Likewise, in scripture, gold often speaks of purity and refinement. When applied to the church we are seeing a vision of a renewed, revived and glorified church.

So the essence of the vision is this: even in times of apostasy, God will have a remnant.

> 1 Kings 19:18: "Yet I will leave seven thousand in Israel, all the knees that have not bowed to Baal, and every mouth that has not kissed him."

God was promising to restore, his people,

his land, the city of Jerusalem and the temple. In New Testament terms, this means:

- I (Jesus) will build my church...
- The church will be a bride without spot or blemish.

A few years ago someone wrote a popular book: "They like Jesus but not the church." This is a popular notion – the idea that we can love Jesus but not the church. The churches have many problems, but it's impossible to love the Lord and not love his church. When the Lord awakens us, he doesn't just birth within us a love for him – he implants a love for his people. We are called to be part of his people and his mission.

The church is Christ's body on earth: the church carries the presence of Christ, does the work of Christ, grows in the character of Christ and is empowered by the Spirit of Christ.

God showed Zerubbabel a vision of the church and asked him, "What do you see?"When you look at your local church, what do you see? When you look at your village, town or city, what do you see?

Do you see:

- A spiritual wasteland or fields white for harvest?
- Problems or possibilities?
- Impossibilities or potential?

I'm not talking about naïve optimism; I'm talking about a hope which is grounded in the purpose and promises of God: 'I *will* build my church…'

You, your church, and your community, are pregnant with potential!

But, in order to grow, we need to go because, "The church that does not evangelise, will fossilise." (Oswald. J. Smith) Jesus tells us to: "Go into all the world…" That is not a suggestion – it's a command!

3) We need a vision of our own unique place within God's purpose

> *[7] And he shall bring forward the top stone amid shouts of 'Grace, grace to it!'" [8] Then the word of the Lord came to me, saying, [9] "The hands of Zerubbabel have laid the foundation of this house; his hands shall also complete it. Then you will know that the Lord of hosts has sent me to you. [10] For whoever has despised the day of small things shall rejoice, and shall see the plumb line in the hand of Zerubbabel.*

Zerubbabel is given a vision of his place within God's purpose, "he shall bring forward the top stone." Each of us also has a unique purpose in God's house. We all have different gifts.

> [18]But as it is, God arranged the members in the body, each one of them, as he chose. 19 If all were a single member, where would the body be? [20] As it is, there are many

parts, yet one body. (1 Cor. 12)

The Bible is clear: we all have gifts, and we don't all have the same gifts. Not all are preachers and teachers. Some have been called to compassion ministries – helping the homeless, people caught in addiction, trauma victims etc. Others are called to be administrators. Others are called to be evangelists.

When you look at your life, in God, 'What do you see?' Do you see your role as insignificant? If you do – you need to change your thinking! Every member, every function, and every gift is important to God and the wellbeing of the church.

[10] For whoever has despised the day of small things?

When we look at our gifts, roles, or our church, the Lord says do not despise the day of small things. Don't see yourself as insignificant. Don't look down on your gifts and calling. God is in the business of taking that which seems insignificant and doing something great with it! The critics said of Jesus: "Can anything good come out of Nazareth?" He takes that which appears small and foolish and transforms it into something wise and glorious – remember the boy with the loaves and the fish? He takes that which is considered shameful and despised and gives it a place of honour and glory – think of the cross.

If your life, from your perspective, is marked by shame, brokenness, and insignificance – you are exactly the kind of material that the Lord delights in using to build something beautiful. If on the other hand, we see ourselves as significant, successful, and strong – we are not much use to the Lord. We need to be broken: "Unless a grain of wheat falls to the ground and dies…"

4) Revival and renewal is inseparable from a fresh vision of Jesus Christ and the gospel

Zerubbabel's role was to lay the foundation and build the house. Revival – or personal salvation – is all about restoring right foundations. The reason we need salvation and revival, is because our foundations are wrong. Without Christ we are building our lives on an illusion. From a New Testament perspective, a true foundation is a life that is built upon Jesus Christ, and His Word.

> "For no one can lay a foundation other than that which is laid, which is Jesus Christ." 1 Cor 3:11

As the hymn writer put it: "On Christ the Solid rock I stand, all other ground is sinking sand"

For the unbeliever, the question is, is your life built upon Jesus Christ? He is the only solid foundation. And the question for every local church is the same: *Are we built upon the foundation of Jesus Christ?*

As churches we can try and build on many good things – gifts, personalities, worship bands, social activities – but when the storms come – none of these things will hold a church together. Only a church built on Christ will stand and flourish.

5) Revival and renewal results in a fresh vision of the lost

Zechariah's prophecy includes a vision of the unbelieving world.

> *Zech 2:11 And many nations shall join themselves to the Lord in that day, and shall be my people. And I will dwell in your midst, and you shall know that the Lord of hosts has sent me to you.*

This is pointing forward to the time of Christ when gentiles would be incorporated into the people of God. The prophetic word to the Jewish nation was always intended to lift their eyes from themselves to the unbelieving nations. They were to be a 'light to the nations.'

'Successful' churches face many dangers. Big churches can be deceived into thinking all is well. It's great that some churches are almost at capacity. It's great when someone plants a church and it takes off! However, it is tempting to think – "man, this is awesome, we've done it – we've planted a church and it's grown to a nice size."

That's the DANGER ZONE!

Let's take an example from my own city – the city of Stirling. The 2012 census estimate for the population of the city is 36,440; the wider Stirling council area has a population of about 93,750. If Stirling reflects the national average, only about 4% of the population in Stirling will have saving faith in Christ. (Approximately just between 3-4000 people.) Basically that means there are approximately 90,000 people to be reached.

When you look at your town or city, and your own spheres of influence, **'What do you see?'**

- Indifference to the gospel?
- Hostility towards the gospel?
- Hard ground?

Zechariah is reminded that the unbelieving nations are to be included in God's promise; we need to be reminded of Jesus words:

> John 4:35: "Do you not say, 'There are yet four months, then comes the harvest'? Look, I tell you, lift up your eyes, and see that the fields are white for harvest."

Throughout our communities there are those who are ready to receive Jesus, now.

When you look at your village, town or city, and your own spheres of influence, 'What do you see?'

I'll tell you what I see—I see churches all over the country where:

- The Homeless find hope and homes
- Drug addicts find deliverance
- Marriages are mended
- The poverty-stricken find provision – and prosperity
- The sick are healed
- The lost are found and sinners are saved

- The saved are set free, equipped and sent into the market place as a light for Christ
- Church is a place where God is found.

I'm not intending to downplay the difficulties: by nature, people are spiritually dead; without Christ we are blind; prior to the new birth we have a heart of stone. However, one of the biggest obstacles to reaching people is our own fear—fear of rejection. Put simply, one of the greatest obstacles to reaching people is the fact that many of us are too afraid to speak to people about Jesus.

Yet, we need to remember that God himself will remove the obstacles:

> *[7]Who are you, O great mountain? Before Zerubbabel you shall become a plain.*

The apostle Peter knew what it was to crumble in fear before the mountain of opposition. Three times he denied Christ. Yet this same Peter is the same apostle who went on to preach Christ boldly on the day of Pentecost.

Perhaps there are mountains in our lives?

Maybe there are mountains of personal difficulty which are blocking out the wider purposes of God? If this is the case, remember: the Lord can remove it, or get us through it—either way he is in the business of dealing with mountains!

6) The Holy Spirit is the one who brings about revival and renewal

⁶ Then he said to me, "This is the word of the LORD to Zerubbabel: Not by might, nor by power, but by my Spirit, says the LORD of hosts.

The Holy Spirit is the one who births, sustains and revives the church. The same is true for the individual. The Holy Spirit brings us to faith in Christ, sustains us and revives us.

The Holy Spirit enables us to witness for Christ:

Acts 1:18 "But you will receive power when the Holy Spirit has come upon you, and you will be my witnesses in Jerusalem and in all Judea and Samaria, and to the end of the earth."

The filling of the Holy Spirit is on-going. Paul tells the Ephesian church 'Be filled with the Holy Spirit.' The same believers who received the Holy Spirit on the day of Pentecost needed to be filled afresh a few days later. We see this because in Acts it tells us that when they were in prayer 'the place where they were gathered was shaken, and they were all filled with the Holy Spirit.

⁶ Then he said to me, "This is the word of the Lord to Zerubbabel: Not by might, nor by power, but by my Spirit, says the Lord of hosts.

This is a powerful verse! It's a reminder that revival is not a work of the flesh. We can't do God's work in our own strength. Preaching can't be done in our own strength. Evangelism can't be done in our own strength. A church won't grow by human effort alone.

However, it's not a call to passivism or hyper Calvinism.

We need the Holy Spirit, but we must actively make room for him. We must actively welcome him. We must actively depend upon him. He doesn't anoint fresh air – he anoints our words and actions.

7) Revival and Renewal are by grace not human effort

> *[7] And he shall bring forward the top stone amid shouts of 'Grace, grace to it!'"*

God told Zerubbabel that the work of restoration would be complete amidst shouts of grace. There is a beautiful modern hymn that connects the restoration of the church with God's grace:

> "Rise up Church with broken wings, fill this place with songs again, of our God who reigns on high, by his grace again we'll fly."

Revival is not a question of us working our way up to the heights of God's presence, revival is God coming down.

Salvation is a sovereign work of grace, so is revival – *but* we can respond to God's alarm call, to wake up, and stir ourselves! What does it mean to awaken ourselves? To awaken ourselves is to be stirred to fresh repentance, prayer and surrender.

3
REBUILDING THE HOUSE (JOHN/ACTS)

I recently read the following fascinating quote in an article about William Carey.

At a meeting of Baptist leaders in the late 1700s, a newly ordained minister stood to argue for the value of overseas missions. He was abruptly interrupted by an older minister, who said,

"Young man, sit down! You are an enthusiast. When God pleases to convert the heathen, he'll do it without consulting you or me."

What was happening here? The cultural Christianity of the time conditioned the church to the point were not only was it neglecting mission – it was opposing mission!

The history of the church shows that very often the church needs to come back to basics. The church can often get it wrong. The church can adopt skewed priorities. The church can often lose sight of what the main thing is. The church often finds itself in need of reformation.

During the reformation, the reformers adopted a phrase: *ecclesia reformata, semper reformanda*: the church reformed, always reforming.

The reformers were getting at the fact that the church always has a tendency to head away from the truth and as a result it must always be brought back to the truth – the church must be constantly seeking to reform, revive, and restore itself to spiritual health.

We shouldn't find this issue surprising – Jesus himself encountered the same issue – the biggest problem Jesus encountered was the religious establishment of his day. Jesus said to them, "Is this not the reason you are wrong, because you know neither the Scriptures nor the power of God? Mark 12:24

And so the pattern continues throughout the history of the church. One writer humorously expressed it this way:

> "Christianity started out in Palestine as a fellowship; it moved to Greece and became a philosophy; it moved to Italy and became an institution; it moved to Europe and became a culture; it came to America and became an enterprise." (Sam Pascoe)

In other words, there is always a danger that our Christianity simply reflects the culture around us, instead of us being transformed by the power of the gospel and living counter-cultural lives.

Here are three examples.

1) How we think about righteousness

- We often think this is something we attain, when in fact it's something we already are (IN CHRIST).

- We think it is something we must do, when it is something that is already done. It's a finished work.

- We think it is something we do to get God's favour, when it's something we already enjoy because God loves us.

Having been declared righteous, then, by faith, we have peace toward God through our Lord Jesus Christ, (Rom. 5:1)

2) How we think about mission

- Again we often assume that mission is something missionaries do. The truth is mission is what all Christians are called to participate in.

- Many think it's the role of missionary organisations when it's actually the call of the church.

- Further, there are still some who think it's a thing that happens in foreign lands, when it should happen wherever God has placed us.

3) How we think about church

- It is often assumed that church is the building when in fact it's the people.

- We talk about "going to church" – when in fact we are the church.

- Some think that Church is a particular denomination – yet the reality is, God does not recognise denominations – he didn't start any of them – there is only one true church that transcends sinful human boundaries.

This last point is the one I want to take up in this chapter – what is the church?

Here are some biblical metaphors:

- Body of Christ
- Bride of Christ
- Family of God
- Temple/House of God

In this chapter, we are going to focus on the last example: House/Temple of God.

The scriptures reveal that God is a House Seeking God.

Most of us will have had the experience of seeking somewhere to live. Maybe it's been as students seeking accommodation; newlyweds seeking their first house or retirees downsizing because the children have flown the nest.

Likewise, in scripture we see that God is looking for a dwelling place – a place to live. It's always been God's purpose to dwell with his people. House/temple is a major theme of scripture; we see it from Genesis to Revelation.

Eden was the place of perfect communion with God.

> Gen 3:8 Then the man and his wife heard the sound of the Lord God as he was walking in the garden in the cool of the day,

But this communion was broken through sin. From Genesis chapter three onwards, the theme is all about God restoring his dwelling place amongst his people.

> Exodus 29:45: "I will dwell among the sons of Israel and will be their God.
>
> Ezekiel 37:27: "My dwelling place also will be with them; and I will be their God, and they will be My people.
>
> Revelation 21:3: And I heard a loud voice from the throne, saying, "Behold, the tabernacle of God is among men, and He will dwell among them, and they shall be His people, and God Himself will be among them

From Exodus to settling in the Promised Land, the Lord dwelt with his people in a tent/tabernacle, with the ark of the covenant being the focal point of his presence.

The LORD gave very specific instructions about the tabernacle:

> Exodus 25:40 "Be sure that you make everything according to the pattern I have shown you here on the mountain."

Then, in 2 Chron 3:1 "Solomon began to build the temple of the Lord in Jerusalem on Mount Moriah, where the Lord had appeared to his father David." And later in 2 Chron. 6:1, 'Then Solomon said, "I have built a magnificent temple for you, a place for you to dwell forever." Yet – despite the glory of the temple – Solomon expresses real spiritual insight:

> **18** "But will God really dwell on earth with humans? The heavens, even the highest heavens, cannot contain you. How much less this temple I have built!

He recognises that God's purpose is to dwell with people and he recognises that this temple of bricks and mortar just can't cut it!

This helps us understand the following passage from Acts:

> **48** "However, the Most High does not live in houses made by human hands. As the prophet says:
>
> **49** "'Heaven is my throne,
> and the earth is my footstool.
> What kind of house will you build for me?
> says the Lord.
> Or where will my resting place be?
> **50** Has not my hand made all these things?'

This is not a contradiction.

What we see here is that the Old Testament Tabernacle and Temple pointed forward to something greater. These things were types and shadows – not the substance and reality.

What the New Testament ultimately reveals is that:

1. The House of God is not the steeple, it's the People

God's House is not the physical building; it's the community of believers.

The New Testament never uses the word church to describe buildings – it is only used to describe the community of believers.

> 2 Corinthians 6:16: Or what agreement has the temple of God with idols? For we are the temple of the living God; just as God said, "I WILL DWELL IN THEM AND WALK AMONG THEM; AND I WILL BE THEIR GOD, AND THEY SHALL BE MY PEOPLE.

Peter teaches the same thing:

You yourselves like living stones are being built up as a spiritual house, to be a holy priesthood, to offer spiritual sacrifices acceptable to God through Jesus Christ. 1 Peter 2:5

Jesus himself introduced this shift in

thinking regarding the temple.

> "Sir," the woman said, "I can see that you are a prophet. Our fathers worshiped on this mountain, but you Jews claim that the place where we must worship is in Jerusalem." Jesus declared, "Believe me, woman, a time is coming when you will worship the Father **neither on this mountain nor in Jerusalem**... Yet a time is coming and has now come when the **true worshipers will worship the Father in spirit and truth**, for they are the kind of worshipers the Father seeks. God is spirit, and his worshipers must worship in spirit and in truth." John 4:19-24 (NIV)

This was a radical concept that Jesus was introducing.

Worship, for the Jew, was all about Jerusalem and the temple – yet here Jesus is altering the playing field. I take Jesus to mean: it's not a question of whether we worship in a cathedral or a cave – the question is: is our worship scriptural (truth) and is it *in* the Holy Spirit? The question is – are we worshipping in spirit and truth? Are we worshipping God the Father, through the Son, in the power of the Holy Spirit? That's what matters.

2. God's House is not about Religious pretence, it's about the Spirit's Presence

In the verses that follow his message in Acts 7, Stephen moves on to a pointed application:

> [51] "You stiff-necked people! Your hearts and ears are still uncircumcised. You are just like your ancestors: You always resist the Holy Spirit!

What's going on here? The religious establishment is opposing the church of Jesus Christ. They think they're the righteous ones. They're all about the temple, rituals, the law, and the traditions of the elders. They saw Jesus as a troublemaker, had him killed – and thought they'd dealt with the Jesus problem.

Now, in the same way that Jesus did, Stephen is calling them out for their religious hypocrisy.

> [51] "You stiff-necked people! Your hearts and ears are still uncircumcised. You are just like your ancestors: You always resist the Holy Spirit!

What's he saying? He is saying, they might be physically circumcised – but their ears and hearts aren't. They may have performed an outward religious duty – but their ears are deaf to God's Word and their hearts are unresponsive to him.

Stephen gets to the root of the issue – "you always resist the Holy Spirit!"

Do we see the contrast?

Jesus says true worship is in "Spirit and truth but the 'religious' worship was resistant to the Spirit, and it was falsehood – a facade. I think one of the reasons why so many people in Scotland – and the western world, have abandoned the church is because they see through the religious façade. The world can smell hypocrisy a mile off.

BUT what happens in seasons of renewal – when the Holy Spirit brings a season of refreshing to the church? People are drawn. The lost return because they see there is something real.

There is a great gulf between self-righteousness and true righteousness. True righteousness is a fruit of the Holy Spirit, false righteousness is from the flesh. You know – most of the conflict and division that I see in the church comes from self-righteousness. Self-righteous people will always oppose the people of the Spirit – because their freedom is a threat.

Don't get me wrong, the House of God is a highway of holiness, but it's also a hospital for those who need to be made whole.

[3]"A bruised reed He will not break, and a dimly burning wick He will not extinguish (Isa 42:3)

Do you ever feel that you are unworthy to worship? Do you ever feel you are a hypocrite because of your ungodliness? His blood flowed for your forgiveness, and His Spirit is here for your cleansing.

The hymn writer reminds us of this powerful truth: "What can wash away my sin? What can make me whole again – Nothing but the blood of Jesus." It's not the healthy who need a doctor, but the sick – likewise, Jesus has come not for the righteous but for sinners.

The presence of God literally dwelt in the temple. Paul is teaching that the presence of God now literally dwells in us, individually and collectively, as believers.

In the Old Testament, after Solomon built and dedicated the temple we read about God's glory filling the temple:

> "In unison when the trumpeters and the singers were to make themselves heard with one voice to praise and to glorify the LORD, and when they lifted up their voice accompanied by trumpets and cymbals and instruments of music, and when they praised the LORD saying,"He indeed is good for His lovingkindness is everlasting," then the house, the house

of the LORD, was filled with a cloud, 14so that the priests could not stand to minister because of the cloud, for the glory of the LORD filled the house of God."

When a person is born again, when a person is filled with the Holy Spirit – the very same presence of God comes into our life.

Now, some of us are very aware when this happens. We can identify with Wesley's words:

> Long my imprisoned spirit lay. Fast bound in sin and nature's night; Thine eye diffused a quickening ray, I woke, the dungeon flamed with light; My chains fell off, my heart was free, I rose, went forth, and followed Thee.

But this is not the case for all of us. For others, it's more like the following example.

In the Old Testament – Jacob has a dream where he sees a ladder bridging heaven and earth and angels ascending and descending.

Then we read –

16Then Jacob awoke from his sleep and said, **"Surely the LORD is in this place, and I did not know it."** 17He was afraid and said, **"How awesome is**

this place! This is none other than the house of God, and this is the gate of heaven."

Jacob was at the place where God was. But he didn't perceive it. He was at house of God but missed the reality of it. He was at the very gate of heaven, yet his eyes were closed to the glory of it.

This can be true of us. We can be blind to the glory that is in us.

Paul uses this phrase to describe what it is to be a Christian: "Christ in you, the hope of glory." This can be true of us, but we can lack an awareness, or assurance of this divine reality.

The Lord said, "Where two or three are gathered in my name, there am I in the midst of them." Yet the truth is we can gather and be conscious of everything and anything other than Christ.

Some worry is weighing upon our mind – yet Christ is here – but we fail to sense his nearness. Or perhaps someone has annoyed us, and we are nursing the grievance – yet the Lord is here and we perceive it not.

This is the battle. This is the battle we all face. It's not that you are less spiritual than anyone else – it's the battle between the flesh and the spirit. This is why Paul prays for the church with these words:

> [18] I ask that the eyes of your heart may be enlightened, so that you may know the hope of His calling, the riches of His glorious inheritance in the saints, [19] and the surpassing greatness of His power to us who believe. He displayed this power in the working of His mighty strength, [20] which He exerted in Christ when He raised Him from the dead and seated Him at His right hand in the heavenly realms, [21] far above all rule and authority, power and dominion, and every name that is named, not only in this age, but also in the one to come.
>
> [22] And God put everything under His feet and made Him head over everything for the church, [23] which is His body, the fullness of Him who fills all in all.

3. In God's house there is no Clergy/Laity divide – every Believer is a priest!

In terms of entering the Holy place – in the Old Testament – only the high priest could enter once a year. Only the tribe of Levites could serve as priests in the temple. However, In the New Testament all believers are priests!

> But you *are* a chosen generation, a royal **priesthood**, a holy nation, His own

special people, that you may proclaim the praises of Him who called you out of darkness into His marvelous light. 1 Peter 2:9

This raises the question – if the house of God is not a physical building – how do we build the church? If we are like living stones being built into a temple – what does it mean for the house of God to be built?

I think the answer lies in 1 Cor. 12-14 and Eph 4.

[4] I therefore, a prisoner for the Lord, urge you to walk in a manner worthy of the calling to which you have been called, [2] with all humility and gentleness, with patience, bearing with one another in love, [3] eager to maintain the unity of the Spirit in the bond of peace. [4] There is one body and one Spirit—just as you were called to the one hope that belongs to your call— [5] one Lord, one faith, one baptism, [6] one God and Father of all, who is over all and through all and in all. [7] But grace was given to each one of us according to the measure of Christ's gift. [8] Therefore it says,

"When he ascended on high he led a host of captives,
 and he gave gifts to men."

⁹ (In saying, "He ascended," what does it mean but that he had also descended into the lower regions, the earth? ¹⁰ He who descended is the one who also ascended far above all the heavens, that he might fill all things.) **¹¹ And he gave the apostles, the prophets, the evangelists, the shepherds and teachers, ¹² to equip the saints for the work of ministry,** for building up the body of Christ, ¹³ until we all attain to the unity of the faith and of the knowledge of the Son of God, to mature manhood, to the measure of the stature of the fullness of Christ, ¹⁴ so that we may no longer be children, tossed to and fro by the waves and carried about by every wind of doctrine, by human cunning, by craftiness in deceitful schemes. ¹⁵ Rather, speaking the truth in love, we are to grow up in every way into him who is the head, into Christ, ¹⁶ from whom the whole body, joined and held together by every joint with which it is equipped, when each part is working properly, makes the body grow so that it builds itself up in love.

- Every believer has a calling (v1)
- God has given the church leadership giftings (apostles, prophets, evangelists, pastors and teachers) (v11)

- The purpose of the leadership giftings is to *equip the saints for the work of ministry* (v12)

- As believers are equipped and released in their calling and ministry – the body of Christ is built up (the church is built).

In practice this looks like –

- Unity of faith
- Fullness of/in Christ
- Stability
- Discernment
- Maturity
- A loving, serving church

So how do we build the church? We discover the spiritual gifts that God has given us and use them for the good of the church and the mission of God.

Final thoughts

We've compared the difference between the House of God in the Old Testament and in the New Testament. It's important to stress that the differences aren't trivial. For some reason – the way we are wired – we have a tendency as God's people to focus on the wrong things. When we think of church primarily as either buildings or denominations – we lose sight of the glorious fact that the Lord's church is his people. It's people that matter to God – not buildings, traditions, or denominations. In other words – it's about ***relationship not religion.***

God is seeking a house – the question is will we be that house?

> *Behold, I stand at the door and knock. If anyone hears my voice and opens the door, I will come in to him and eat with him, and he with me. 3:20*

4

CAN THESE BONES LIVE? (EZEKIEL 37)

*The hand of the Lord was on me, and he brought me out by the Spirit of the Lord and set me **in the middle of a valley**; it **was full of bones**. ² He led me back and forth among them, and I saw a great many bones on the floor of the valley, **bones that were very dry**.*

Let's consider the setting of our passage – here we have a prophet who finds himself in *a valley*, which is *full of bones* – and *very dry!* The imagery is very powerful – he's in a valley – valleys often speak of depression, darkness and defeat.

In times of battle, it is a disadvantage to

be in the valley – the vantage point is the mountain top. God's people are in a battle – and very often it can feel like we are in the valley – the Christian life can feel like an uphill struggle. The mountain top is the place of vision, victory and exaltation, but the valley is the place of struggle, shadows, and limited perspective.

The valley is full of bones – in other words, it is a place of death. Instead of life, and vibrancy, the valley is immersed in death. That can be our experience too, Jesus has said: "I have come that you may have life, and life in all its fullness" yet sometimes, even as Christians, we can feel more dead than we do alive.

Further, the bones were *very dry* – again this is the opposite imagery of blessing. God's blessing is often expressed in terms of outpouring, refreshing and streams of living water.

> For I will pour water on the thirsty land, and streams on the dry ground; I will pour my Spirit upon your offspring, and my blessing on your descendants. (Psalm 44:3)

> "Whoever believes in me, as the Scripture has said, 'Out of his heart will flow rivers of living

water.'" (John 7:38)

However, here the prophet is in the place of dryness – his experience is more like the psalmist who cried out:

> "O God, you are my God; earnestly I seek you; my soul thirsts for you; my flesh faints for you, as in a dry and weary land where there is no water." (Psalm 63:1)

How would we describe our present spiritual life? Are we in a place of refreshing, or are we in a place of barrenness and dryness?

But what is this vision of the valley all about? The valley of dry bones is a picture of the nation of Israel.

At the time of the prophet Ezekiel, Israel had been taken into Babylonian Captivity. To all intents and purposes, the nation of Israel was dead. They had lost their land, their city of Jerusalem and their temple. Consequently, their hope was dead and it seemed like God's purpose for their nation was also dead.

In many ways, it's a similar picture of today's church. We may not be in physical/geographical captivity, but we are certainly in moral and spiritual captivity. The church, instead of being in a place of national life, energy and blessing – in many places looks dead or dying.

We could also apply this to my own nation – Scotland – or Britain – in terms of its historical identity as a 'Christian Nation'. Scotland has been referred to as 'The Land of the Book' or more recently Tom Lennie wrote a book calling Scotland 'The land of Revivals'. David Cameron claimed recently that 'Britain is a 'Christian Nation.'" Anyway, for over 1500 years our nation was identified with Christianity – the Word of God underpinned the laws and social culture of the land.

We are like the nation of Israel here, in the sense that we have been a nation built upon the Word of God and knew the blessing of God, and we are now a nation who has wandered from God – rejected God – and are under the judgement of God.

So the valley of Dry bones is literally the nation of Israel. But in applying this passage – we can think about it:

- Individually – in terms of our own relationship with God.
- Collectively – in terms of the church of God.
- Nationally – in terms of the UK as a post-Christian Nation.
- Christologically – In the light of Redemption.

Standing in the valley of death, defeat and depression – God speaks to the prophet:

> *³ He asked me, "Son of man, can these bones live?"*

And that is a question we should be thinking of when we think of the church in the western world, Scotland, and our local community – our own spiritual lives – or the lives of those we know who are outside of Christ – "can these bones live?"

Can I know something of the Spirit's reviving in my life? Can our nation be restored to righteousness? Can the church be revived, reformed and renewed? Can the prodigals return? Can the lost be found? Can these bones live?

The prophet's response to God is filled with wisdom – "I said, "Sovereign Lord, you alone know."

It's good to recognise, whatever season we are in as individuals, local churches or a nation – that God is sovereign. He is the God of the mountain top and the valley. Whether we are in a season of revival, or apostasy, God is on the throne.

Notice *who* it is that brought the prophet into the valley – "The hand of the Lord was on me, *and he brought me* out *by the Spirit of the Lord* and set me *in the middle of a valley."*

It is God who brought the prophet to the valley, and it is God who sent Israel to captivity – likewise it is God who is sovereign over every season of our life. The songwriter expresses it well:

Blessed Be Your Name, In the land that is plentiful. Where Your streams of abundance flow, Blessed be Your name. Blessed Be Your name, When I'm found in the desert place. Though I walk through the wilderness, Blessed Be Your name.

Whilst it is Israel's unfaithfulness that has led to their captivity – which is God's discipline – *God still has a purpose for His people.* God has a purpose, and that purpose is restoration – we see the purpose of God being fulfilled 10 years later – we see the prophets Haggai, and Zechariah – prophesying that the time of restoration has come.

We know that the bones would in

fact come to life again. The Minor Prophets show us the restoration of the temple, the city and the nation.

Whilst God is Sovereign – this passage in Ezekiel shows us three essential factors in the process of restoration.

1. The Proclamation of the Word of God
2. The Receiving of the Spirit of God
3. The mobilisation of the people of God

1. The Proclamation of the Word of God

(4) Then he said to me, "Prophesy to these bones and say to them, 'Dry bones, hear the word of the Lord!

Our greatest need, as individuals, as a church, or as a nation, is to hear the word of the Lord!

It's good that we gather as the church – in many ways it is an indication that we want to hear the Word of the Lord. And preachers have a responsibility to make sure they preach the word of the Lord!

> Preach the word; be ready in season and out of season; reprove, rebuke, and exhort, with complete patience and teaching.

(2 Tim 4:2)

Whilst, the preacher has *a responsibility to preach* – the congregation has a responsibility to receive the Word of the Lord. Yet because of our sinful nature, we have the capacity to deceive ourselves – we can be in the very place where the Word is being preached, yet we can be stone deaf to it. This is why Jesus repeatedly said – "He who has ears to hear, let him hear."

What is God's solution to the valley of dry bones?

> 'Dry bones, *hear the word of the Lord!*

What is God's solution to our own valley of dryness and deadness?

> 'Dry bones, *hear the word of the Lord!*

What is God's solution to a spiritually dead church, nation or sinner?

> 'Dry bones, *hear the word of the Lord!*

The Word of God is life giving! It's the Word of God that can bring reviving and restoration.

> The law of the Lord is perfect, refreshing the soul.

> The statutes of the Lord are trustworthy,
> making wise the simple.
> ⁸ The precepts of the Lord are right,
> giving joy to the heart.
> The commands of the Lord are radiant,
> giving light to the eyes. (Psalm 19)

However, whilst the Word of the Lord has the capacity to restore life – we can see from this passage that something else must accompany the preaching of the Word of the Lord.

> ⁷ So I prophesied as I was commanded. And as I was prophesying, there was a noise, a rattling sound, and the bones came together, bone to bone. ⁸ I looked, and tendons and flesh appeared on them and skin covered them, but there was no breath in them.

The word breath/wind and Spirit are often interchangeable. The meaning seems to be very clear – the Word alone without the Spirit is insufficient.

2. The Receiving of the Spirit of God

> ⁹ Then he said to me, "Prophesy to the breath; prophesy, son of man, and say to it, 'This is what the Sovereign Lord

says: Come, breath, from the four winds and breathe into these slain, that they may live.'" [10] So I prophesied as he commanded me, and breath entered them; they came to life and stood up on their feet—a vast army.

Many of us have assembled in church, week after week, month after month, and year after year. Many in churches will often confess, that whilst they desire to know the assurance of God's power – they cannot help but feel that something is missing. What is it that is missing? It is often the work of the Spirit!

For some people, they *need the initial work of the Spirit* to take place in their life – *they need to be born again* by personally responding to the gospel.

> And it came to pass, that, while Apollos was at Corinth, Paul having passed through the upper coasts came to Ephesus: and finding certain disciples,
>
> [2] He said unto them, Have ye received the Holy Ghost since ye believed? And they said unto him, We have not so much as heard whether there be any Holy Ghost.
>
> [3] And he said unto them, Unto what then were ye baptized? And they said, Unto John's baptism.

⁴ Then said Paul, John verily baptized with the baptism of repentance<u>, saying unto the people, that **they should believe** on him which should come after him, that is, on Christ Jesus.</u>

⁵ When they heard this, they were baptized in the name of the Lord Jesus.

⁶ And when Paul had laid his hands upon them, the Holy Ghost came on them (Acts 19)

If you are reading this book, and you have never personally responded to the Gospel – you have never personally trusted in Christ – this is where you must begin – this is the missing piece of your Christian life.

However, it is also possible, that those of us who are Christians can also lack the work of the Spirit. The work of the Spirit is on-going.

> Eph 1:17 – I keep asking that the God of our Lord Jesus Christ, the glorious Father, may give you the Spirit[f] of wisdom and revelation, so that you may know him better. ¹⁸ I pray that the eyes of your heart may be enlightened in order that you may know the hope to which he has called you, the riches of his glorious inheritance

in his holy people, [19] and his incomparably great power for us who believe.

Paul prays this for Christians – it is possible to be a Christian and lack assurance – the answer is to pray for the Spirit of wisdom and revelation'.

In other words, we pray that the Spirit will help us see who God is and what he has done for us. This is also why elsewhere Paul commands us to be filled with the Spirit.

> "And do not get drunk with wine, for that is debauchery, but be filled with the Spirit" (Eph 5:18)

The work of the Spirit is absolutely essential. If the Word of God is to be made effective in our lives – we must know the working of the Spirit.

The Westminster Shorter Catechism touches on this:

89) Q: How is the word made effectual to salvation?

> **A:** *The Spirit of God* maketh the reading, but especially the preaching of the word an effectual means of convincing

and converting sinners, and of building them up in holiness and comfort through faith unto salvation.

29) Q: How are we made partakers of the redemption purchased by Christ?

A: We are made partakers of the redemption purchased by Christ, by the effectual application of it to us *by his Holy Spirit.*

However, as we read earlier, we can resist the work of the Spirit:

> "You stiff-necked people, uncircumcised in heart and ears, you always resist the Holy Spirit. As your fathers did, so do you. (Acts 7:51)

True believers can grieve the Spirit through unrepentant sin:

> And do not grieve the Holy Spirit of God, by whom you were sealed for the day of redemption. (Eph 4:30)

We can also quench the Holy Spirit – "Do not quench the Spirit." (1 Thess 5:19)

David Robertson once wrote: "If the

Holy Spirit were removed from the church in the UK today I suspect that 90 per cent of what we do would carry on as if nothing had happened!" Robertson goes on to say, "Too much of the British church is without God, without Christ and without the Holy Spirit."

What about us? Are we filled with the Spirit? Are we depending upon the Holy Spirit? Are we led by the Spirit? The Spirit-filled-life is the normal Christian life.

What does a Spirit-filled church look like? Some, in their zeal for the Holy Spirit have turned the church into a circus. They get caught up in mysticism but at a very basic level, the Spirit-filled church is filled with God's presence and power, and manifesting both the gifts and the fruit of the Spirit.

> Gal 5: [22] But the fruit of the Spirit is love, joy, peace, forbearance, kindness, goodness, faithfulness, [23] gentleness and self-control.

In Acts we see a Spirit-filled church – and Luke says, "And the disciples were filled with *joy* and with the Holy Spirit" Acts 13:52)

3. The mobilisation of the people of God

> [10] So I prophesied as he commanded me, and breath entered them; they came to life and stood up on their feet— a vast army.

Notice when the people of God receive the Spirit of God – that they are assembled as a "vast army." It's only when Christ returns and restores all things that the church will become the "Church Triumphant", until then, we are the "Church Militant."

> "In heaven we shall appear, not in armour, but in robes of glory. But here these are to be worn night and day; we must walk, work, and sleep in them, or else we are not true soldiers of Christ." (William Gurnall)

We are the army of God –

> Onward, Christian soldiers, marching as to war,
> With the cross of Jesus going on before.
> Christ, the royal Master, leads against the foe;
> Forward into battle see His banners go!
>
> At the sign of triumph Satan's host doth flee;
> On then, Christian soldiers, on to victory!
> Hell's foundations quiver at the shout of praise;
> Brothers lift your voices, loud your anthems raise.

If we do not see ourselves as being in the battle, perhaps it is because we have not heard the Word of the Lord calling us to war.

When the time actually came for this vision to become a reality – there was a call that came from God to mobilise the people – they **were called to action.** Haggai issued the challenge: – "Is it a time for you yourselves to be living in your panelled houses, while this house remains a ruin?"

And by the time we get to Nehemiah we read, "Those who carried materials did their work with one hand and held a weapon in the other." (Neh. 4:17)

Conclusion

[11] Then he said to me: "Son of man, these bones are the people of Israel. They say, 'Our bones are dried up and our hope is gone; we are cut off.' [12] Therefore prophesy and say to them: 'This is what the Sovereign Lord says: My people, I am going to open your graves and bring you up from them; I will bring you back to the land of Israel. [13] Then you, my people, will know that I am the Lord, when I open your graves and bring you up from them. [14] I will put my Spirit in you and you will live, and I will settle you in your own land. Then you will know that I the Lord have

spoken, and I have done it, declares the Lord.'"

Like all prophetic passages in scripture – there are layers of interpretation. Historically, this passage is about the restoration of the nation of Israel which was fulfilled when Israel returned from Babylonian captivity. We've been applying some of the truths from this passage to our own context. However, there is another essential and crucial way of looking at this passage. We don't just see God's restorative purpose, for the Nation of Israel, but we also see God's Redemptive purpose for his New Testament people – that is the church.

What do we see in this passage? *En masse* death – and a promise of resurrection and life. From God's perspective *this whole world is a valley of dry bones*. Eph 2:15 reveals that outside of Christ we are all "dead in our trespasses and sins" And that it is God who "made us alive with Christ even when we were dead in transgressions."

Jesus is our Prophet who comes and says to us *"Dry Bones hear the Word of the Lord!"* It is Jesus who calls us out of death and into life. It is Jesus who breathes into us the Wind of the Spirit and who says to us – live again!

And all this is *only possible* because he himself entered the valley of death and died our death. Having tasted death on our behalf – he, by the Spirit of God, was raised from death so that he might raise us from death.

This is where all revival, restoration and renewal begins whether it is individually, congregationally or nationally – our only hope lies in the great redemptive work of Christ whose death and resurrection is the only hope for the nations.

In the midst of individual, congregational and national barrenness – let us look to Christ.

ABOUT THE AUTHOR

John Caldwell is married to Laura, has two sons, Ethan and Caleb, and is actively involved in preaching, teaching, local mission, and church-based evangelism.

Printed in Great Britain
by Amazon